T0400787

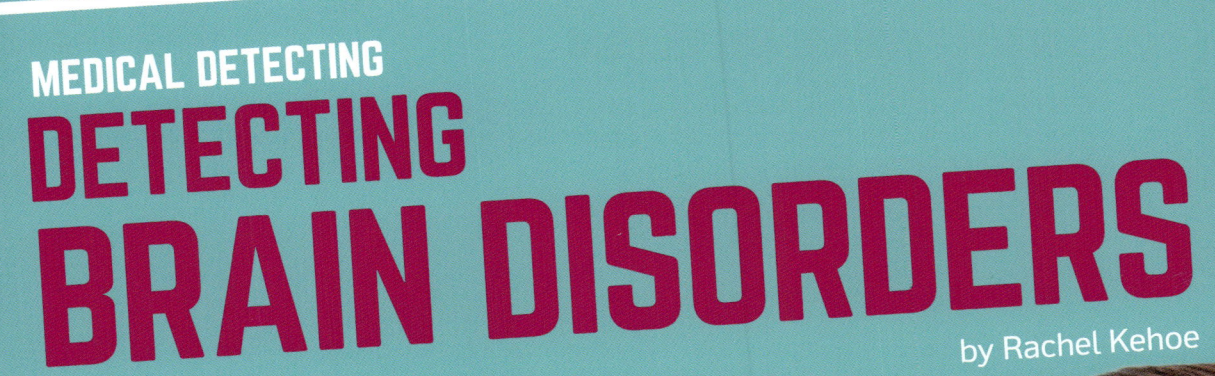

MEDICAL DETECTING

# DETECTING
# BRAIN DISORDERS

by Rachel Kehoe

FOCUS READERS

READERS.

NAVIGATOR

# WWW.FOCUSREADERS.COM

Focus Readers is distributed by North Star Editions:
sales@northstareditions.com | 888-417-0195

Produced for Focus Readers by Red Line Editorial.

Content Consultant: Katie Bullinger, MD/PhD, Assistant Professor of Neurology, Emory University

Photographs ©: Shutterstock Images, cover, 1, 4–5, 6, 8–9, 11, 12–13, 14, 17, 23, 24, 26–27, 29; iStockphoto, 19, 20–21

**Library of Congress Cataloging-in-Publication Data**
Names: Kehoe, Rachel, author.
Title: Detecting brain disorders / by Rachel Kehoe.
Description: Lake Elmo, MN : Focus Readers, [2024] | Series: Medical detecting | Includes index. | Audience: Grades 4-6
Identifiers: LCCN 2023003401 (print) | LCCN 2023003402 (ebook) | ISBN 9781637396223 (hardcover) | ISBN 9781637396797 (paperback) | ISBN 9781637397886 (pdf) | ISBN 9781637397367 (ebook)
Subjects: LCSH: Brain--Imaging--Juvenile literature. | Brain--Diseases--Juvenile literature. | Imaging systems in medicine--Juvenile literature.
Classification: LCC RC386.6.D52 K44 2024  (print) | LCC RC386.6.D52 (ebook) | DDC 616.8/04754--dc23/eng/20230414
LC record available at https://lccn.loc.gov/2023003401
LC ebook record available at https://lccn.loc.gov/2023003402

Printed in the United States of America
Mankato, MN
082023

# ABOUT THE AUTHOR

Rachel Kehoe is a science writer and children's author. She has published several books and articles on science, technology, and climate change. Rachel is interested in research about nutrition and how food impacts health. She calls Ontario, Canada, her home.

# TABLE OF CONTENTS

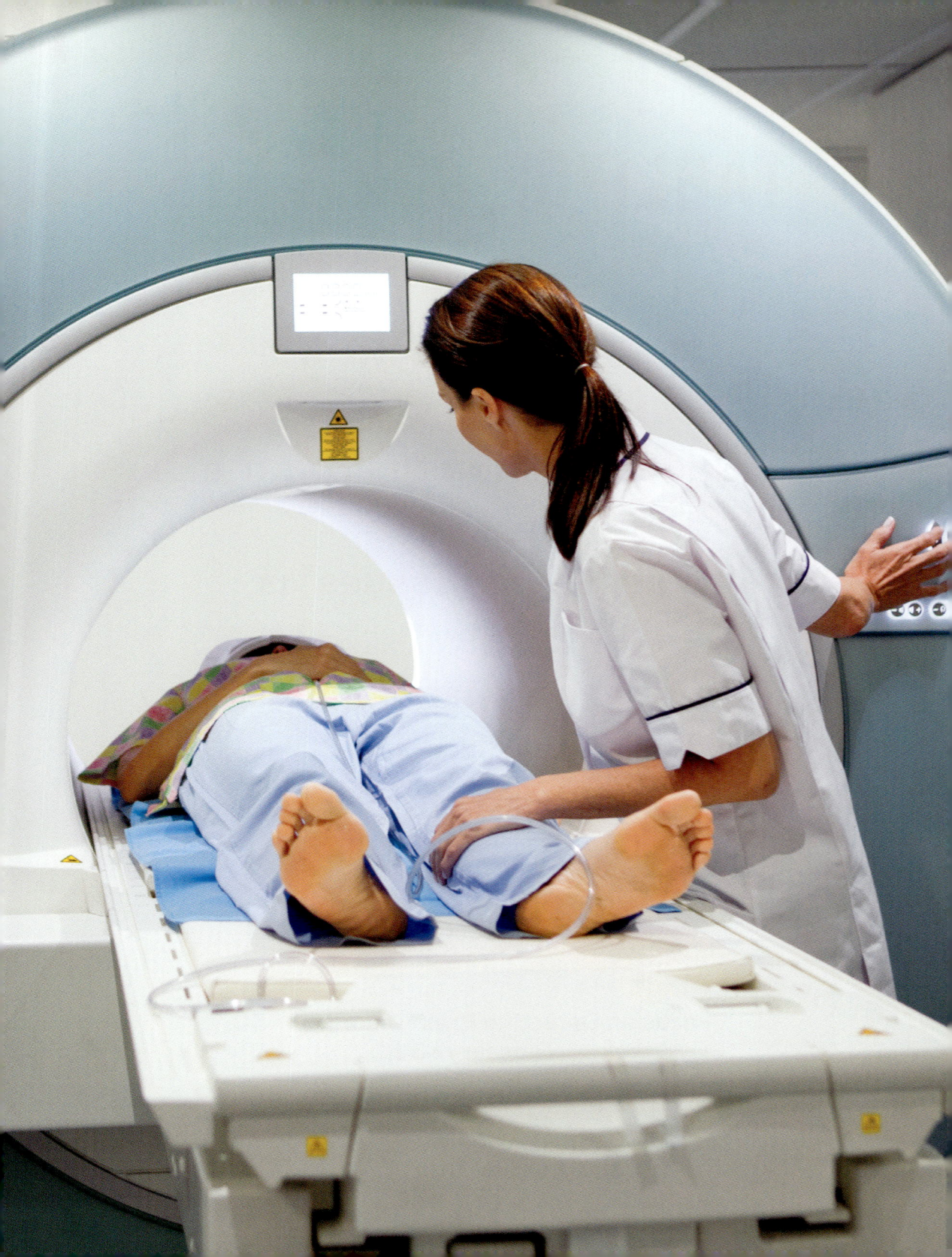

# CHAPTER 1

# GETTING AN MRI

A patient has been having bad headaches. So, her doctor orders an MRI scan. Because MRIs use magnets, the patient can't wear anything metal. She removes her belt and earrings.

The patient also gets an IV. It sends a clear liquid into her blood. This liquid is

**An MRI scanner creates 3D images showing the inside of a patient's body.**

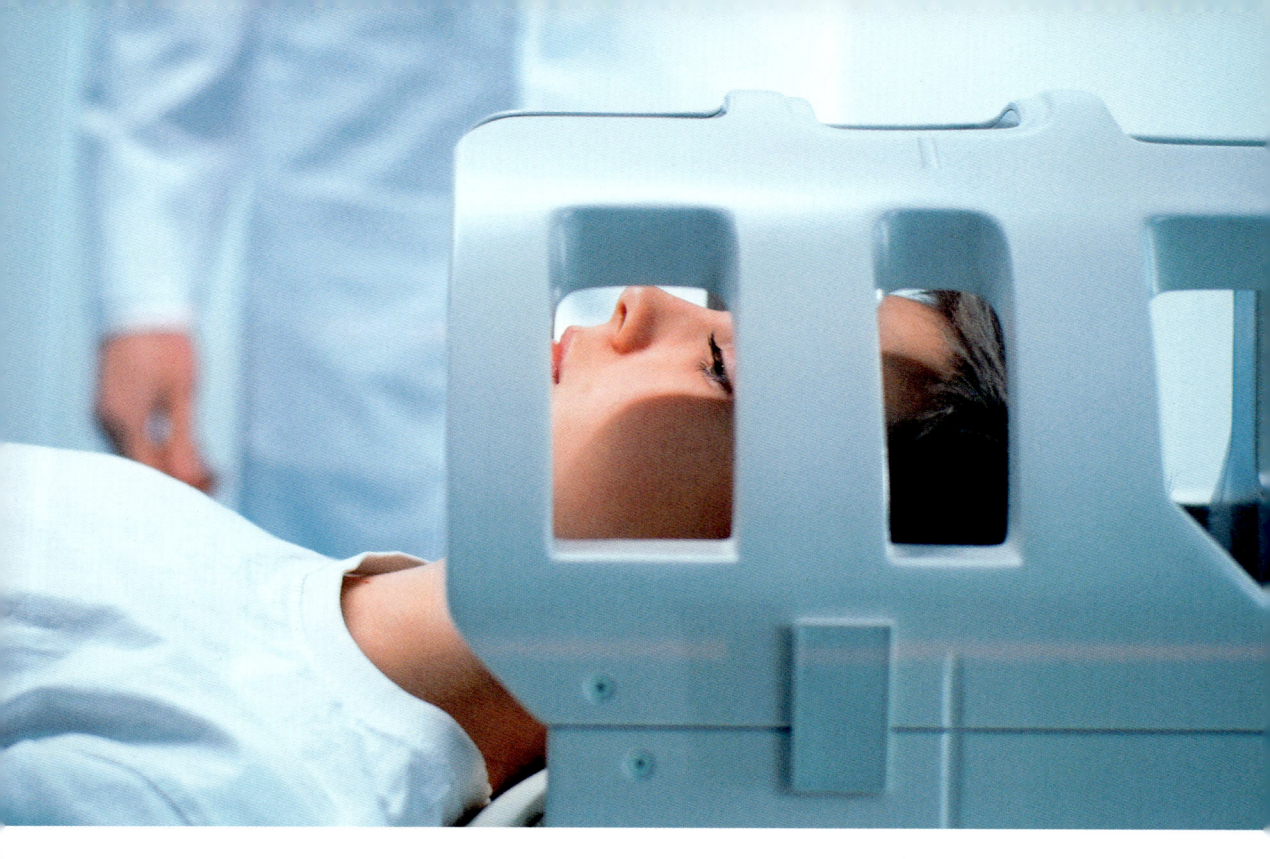

a type of dye. It will help make the scan's image clearer.

Next, the patient walks into the MRI room. She lies down on a flat bed. A coil is placed over her head like a helmet. It sends signals to a computer.

The bed slides into a machine, which looks like a big tunnel. The patient hears loud banging sounds as the scan starts. But this is normal. She holds still so the image won't be blurry.

After a few minutes, the scan is over. The patient's doctor studies the image. He looks for signs of sickness or injury.

## HOW MRIs WORK

An MRI uses a magnetic field and radio waves to send signals. The signals are processed by a computer. It creates a detailed image of the patient's body. This image can show nerve damage, swelling, or bleeding. Doctors often use MRIs to detect problems in the brain.

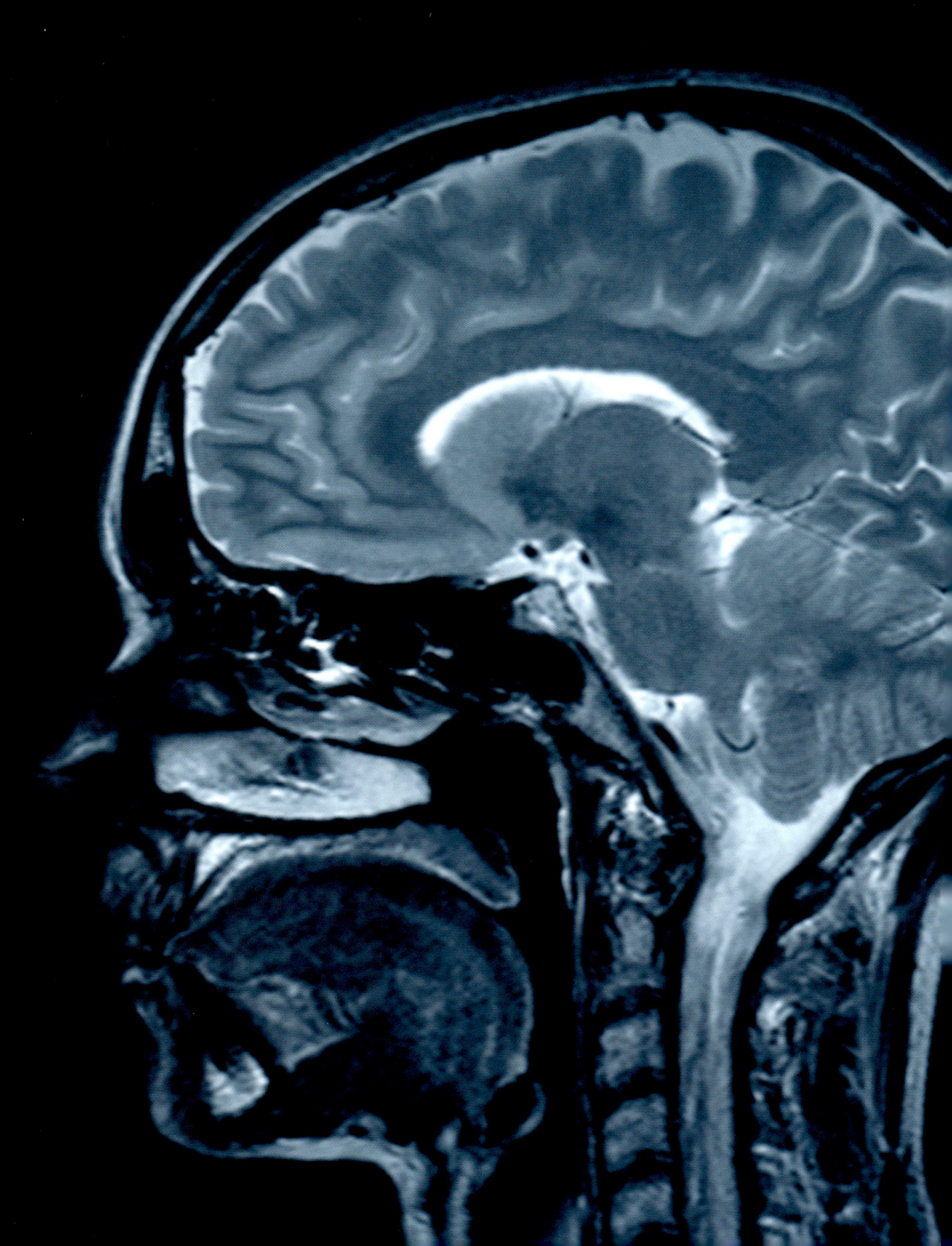

# CHAPTER 2

# UNDERSTANDING THE BRAIN

The brain is part of the nervous system. It acts as the body's control center. It controls a person's senses, muscles, speech, and memory. So, problems in the brain can affect all these things.

There are many kinds of brain disorders. Some are caused by illness. For example, a **tumor** may grow inside

Together, the brain and spinal cord make up the body's central nervous system.

a person's head. Other times, a person's brain is damaged by an injury. Some people are born with brain disorders. These disorders can be **genetic**.

Long ago, doctors could study the brain only after a person had died. But in 1924, a doctor invented the EEG. This machine records the brain's electrical activity. Doctors use EEGs to see how the brain sends signals.

Doctors also developed other types of scans that could show brain tissue. Doctors could now see what people's brains looked like and if they were healthy. In the 1990s, the fMRI was invented. It measures changes in the brain's blood flow. Studying fMRI scans helped doctors learn which parts of the brain were involved with different tasks and activities. The scans also helped doctors **diagnose** brain disorders.

# PARTS OF THE BRAIN

**The brain is divided into several sections. Each part controls different things.**

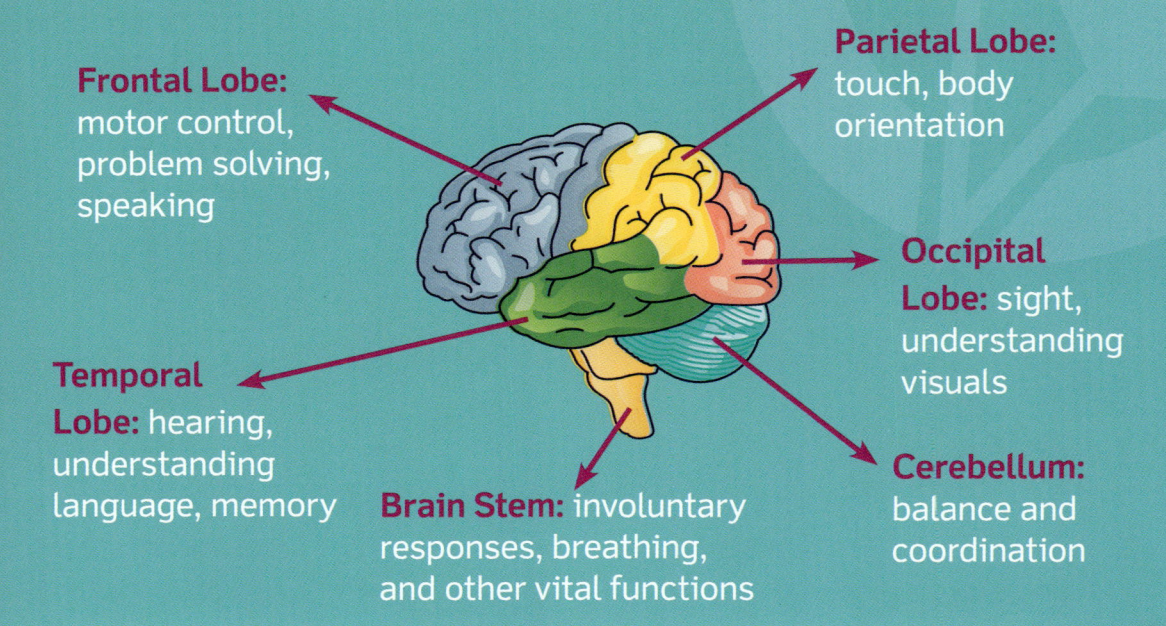

**Frontal Lobe:** motor control, problem solving, speaking

**Parietal Lobe:** touch, body orientation

**Occipital Lobe:** sight, understanding visuals

**Temporal Lobe:** hearing, understanding language, memory

**Brain Stem:** involuntary responses, breathing, and other vital functions

**Cerebellum:** balance and coordination

# CHAPTER 3

# IDENTIFYING ISSUES

Today, doctors have many ways to find problems in the brain. They often begin by talking with patients. They ask about patients' **symptoms**. They ask about previous illnesses or injuries as well. Some types of brain disorders run in families. So, learning each patient's history is important.

After talking with patients, doctors often check how patients' nerves are working.

Next, a doctor may do a neurological exam. This exam tests for brain damage. Doctors ask questions to test patients' thinking and **alertness**. They also check patients' pupils and eye movements. A lack of response can be a sign of damage.

Other parts of the neurological exam check patients' muscles and balance. Doctors may have patients walk in a straight line. Or they may ask patients to lift their arms. These checks can reveal

## CHECKING COGNITION

Cognitive tests check memory and thinking. Patients may be asked to memorize lists of objects. They may also be asked to count or spell backward. People with **dementia** often struggle to do these tests. But so do some patients with strokes, seizures, or tumors. So, the tests don't diagnose disorders. They just reveal problems. Doctors must run other tests to find the cause.

muscle weakness. Doctors may also ask patients to smile, raise their eyebrows, or stick out their tongues. These actions show if the facial muscles are working.

Other types of tests check for nerve damage. For sensory tests, a doctor touches a patient's skin with a small object that pokes or vibrates. The patient describes what they feel. A doctor may also test a patient's **reflexes**. They use a small hammer to tap near the patient's knee. The patient's leg should jerk. The doctor may also tap near wrists, ankles, or elbows. Lack of movement is a sign something is wrong. So is too much movement.

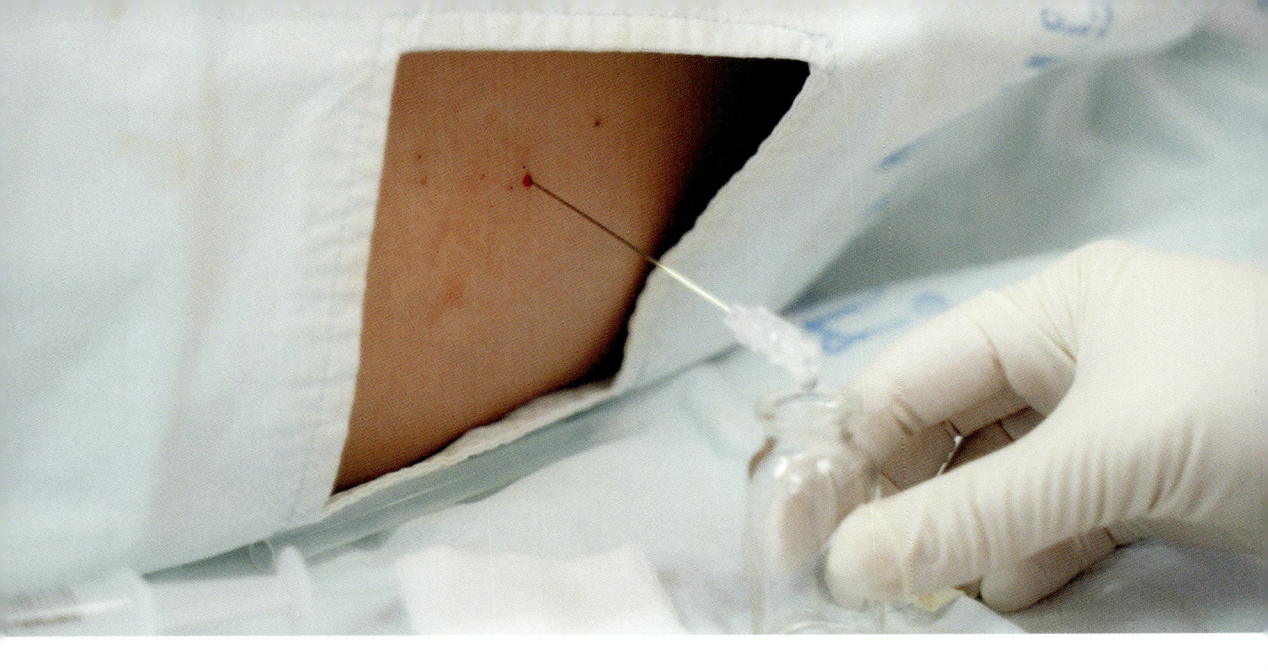

Fluid surrounds the brain and spinal cord to protect them. A spinal tap takes some of this fluid from a person's back.

If doctors find problems, they may do other tests to find the cause. Blood tests can reveal some disorders. For others, doctors use spinal taps. A needle takes fluid from near a patient's spinal cord. This test can find signs of bleeding or infection. Both can cause damage to the brain.

# TESTING FOR ALZHEIMER'S

Alzheimer's disease causes problems with thinking and memory. It is caused by changes in the brain's **proteins**. These changes prevent brain cells from working properly. Over time, the cells die, and the brain shrinks. As a result, the person forgets more and more.

Alzheimer's mainly affects older people. Doctors often diagnose it after people have already begun forgetting things. First, doctors ask patients to do cognitive tests. These tests show how much memory loss a patient has. To learn if Alzheimer's is the cause, doctors do more tests or scans.

Some researchers are developing blood tests to tell if someone has Alzheimer's. These tests

One cognitive test has people draw a clock. People with Alzheimer's struggle to put the numbers in order.

look for certain proteins in the person's blood. These proteins often form before a person begins showing symptoms of the disease. As of 2022, the tests were not widely used. But one day, they might help doctors make earlier diagnoses. Patients could start treatment sooner, which could help slow their memory loss.

# CHAPTER 4

# BRAIN SCANS

When doctors find problems, scans can help identify the cause. CT scans are one example. A CT scanner looks similar to an MRI. But its camera uses X-rays to take a series of pictures. The pictures are combined to make one 3D image. A CT scan is less clear than an MRI. But it is cheaper and faster.

**EEGs only track brain waves. Other scans create images of the brain.**

Some doctors may use CT scans to check for strokes or brain bleeds. That way, they can find and treat the problems quickly. MRIs can show signs or causes of seizures. This can help doctors diagnose **epilepsy**.

For PET scans, a patient is injected with a **radioactive** tracer. This liquid contains sugar. It gathers in the parts of the body that use the most energy. The PET scanner makes a 3D image showing where the tracer ends up. Places with more tracer appear as bright spots. These places can be signs of disease. For example, cancer cells use more sugar than normal cells. So, PET scans can help

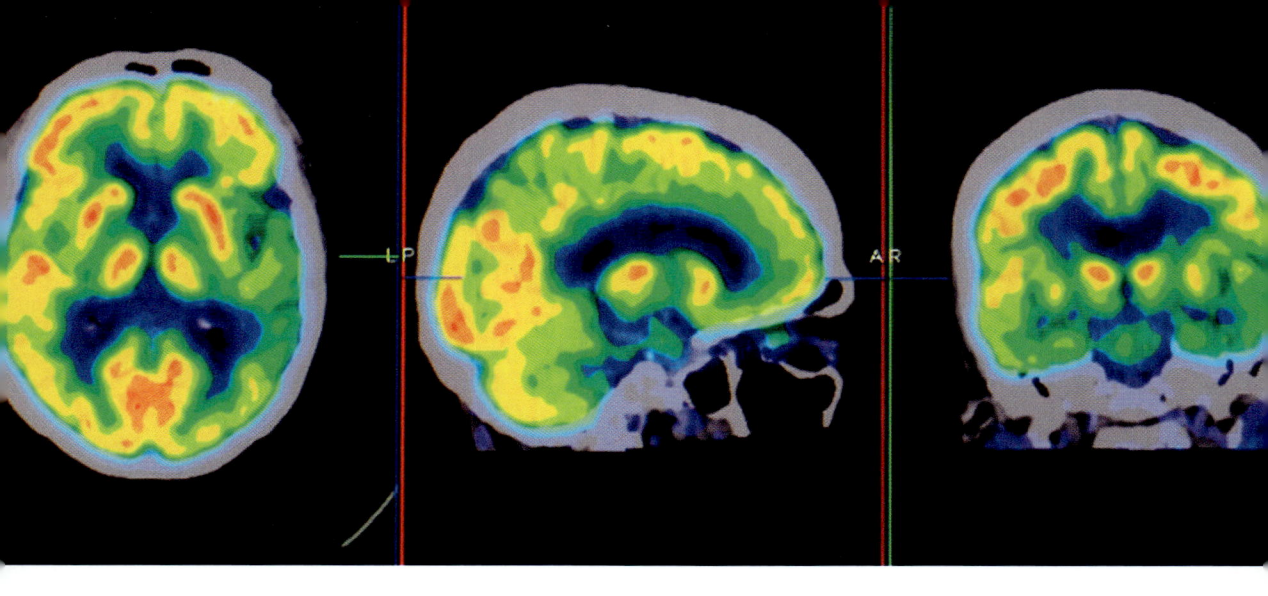

The brain uses sugar for energy. By tracing sugar, a PET scan can show which parts of the brain are active.

doctors find tumors. The scans can also show how disorders affect brain function. By finding small changes, the scans help doctors catch problems at early stages.

A SPECT scan also uses a tracer. This type of scan measures changes in the brain's blood flow. It can find clogged or narrow blood vessels. Both can be signs of disease. SPECT scans can also

show where seizures take place. In some cases, doctors use a type of SPECT scan to confirm if patients have Parkinson's disease. That brain disorder affects movement.

Most brain scans are painless. But they do have some downsides. Some scans are expensive. Also, PET and CT scans both involve radiation. Being exposed to radiation can increase a person's risk of cancer. Some people are allergic to tracers or contrast dyes. But doctors have ways to reduce these reactions. They work to help patients stay safe.

## MENTAL HEALTH

Mental disorders affect how the brain works. They impact how people think, feel, and act. Doctors may use brain scans to rule out other things that could cause similar symptoms. But scans can't diagnose mental health problems. Instead, doctors talk with patients. They find a diagnosis that fits each patient's experience.

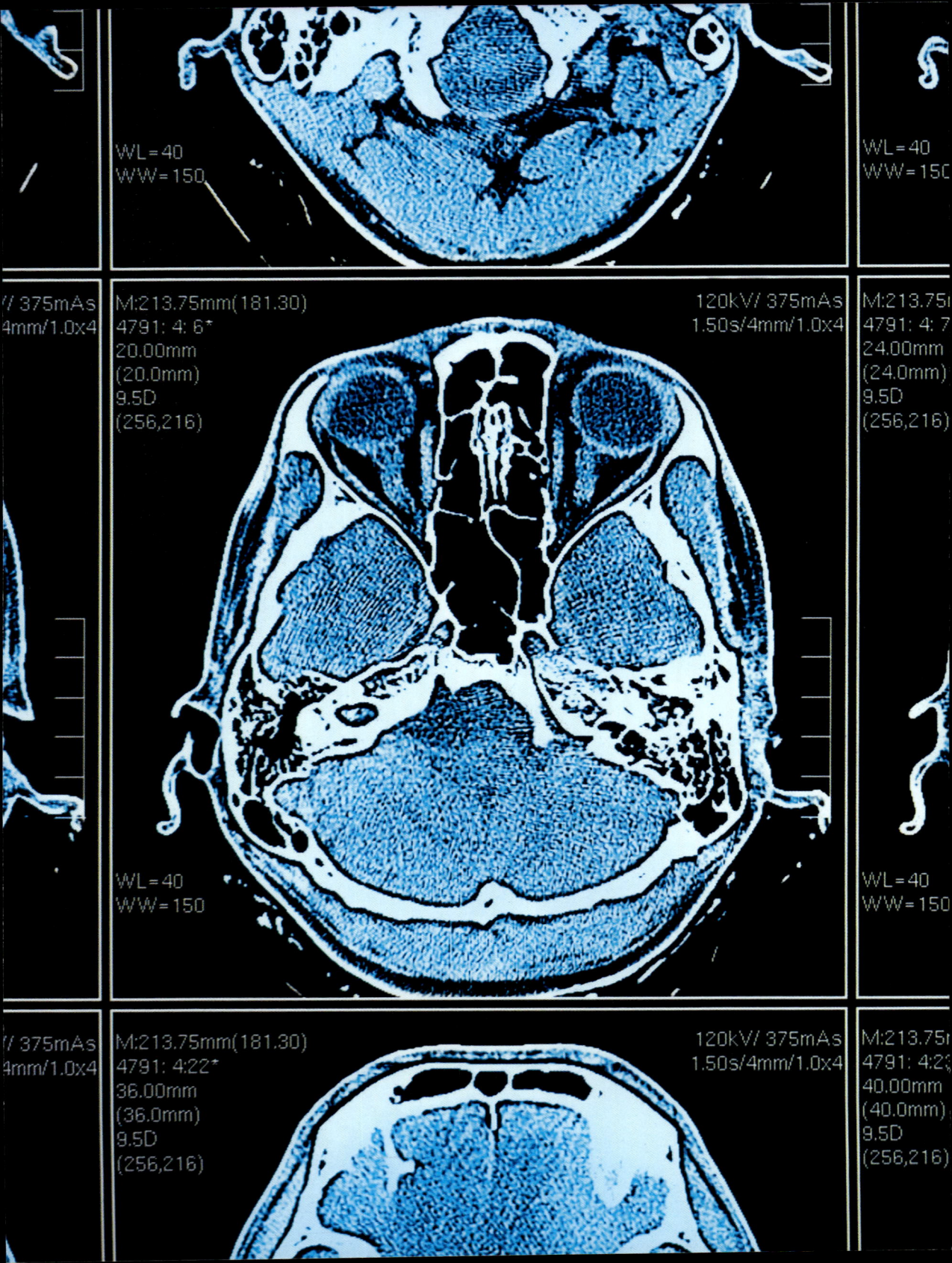

# CHAPTER 5

# NEW BREAKTHROUGHS

Scientists continue to develop new ways to detect brain disorders. In 2021, scientists tested a brain scanning tool called fPACT. A laser beam is pointed at a patient's head. The light causes blood cells to vibrate. Sensors pick up these vibrations. They use the vibrations to make a 3D image.

**Scientists are working to create new types of scans and new ways for computers to study them.**

An fPACT can show many of the same things as an fMRI. But it costs less. It could also work for more patients. As of 2022, the procedure still had challenges. The patient's skull sometimes made the images blurry. Scientists continued working on the tool.

## BETTER MEG

MEG technology measures electrical activity in the brain. It helps doctors find where seizures take place. Many MEG devices are bulky. But researchers are working on smaller devices. These devices look like helmets. They use magnetic sensors. They can adjust to fit the size of each patient's head. They are also more sensitive.

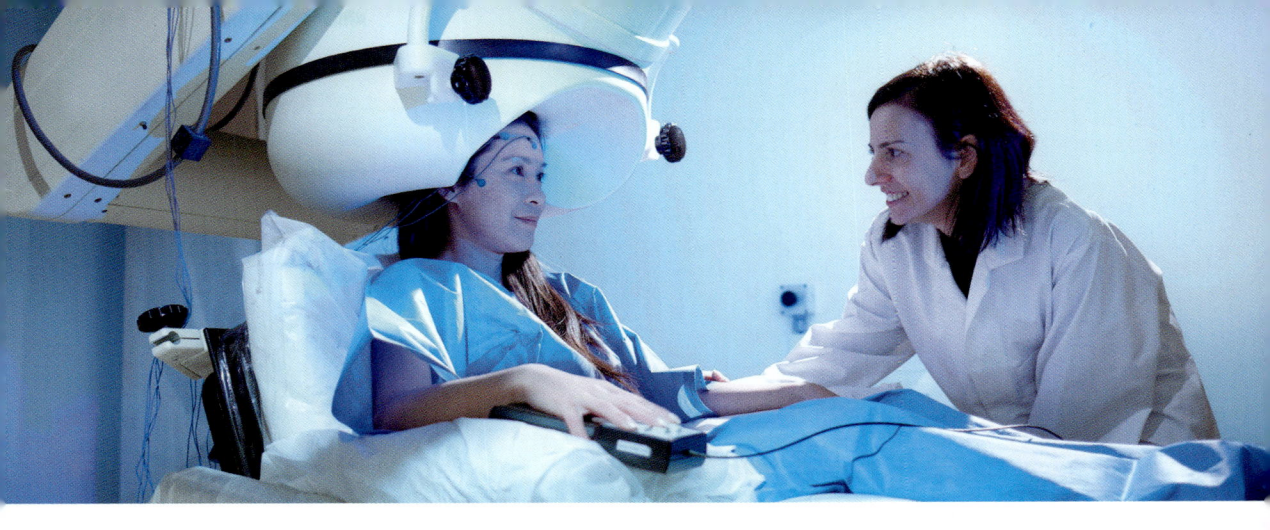

For most MEG devices, patients must hold still and sit under large scanners with wires attached to their heads.

Artificial intelligence (AI) is another research focus. Doctors are already using AI to diagnose some brain disorders. At one hospital, AI examined brain tissue. It studied hundreds of samples from patients with brain disorders. It found tiny changes that showed the start of disease. By finding patterns, AI could help doctors diagnose disorders more quickly and easily.

# DETECTING BRAIN DISORDERS

*Write your answers on a separate piece of paper.*

**1.** Write a paragraph describing one type of brain scan and how it works.

**2.** Which new technology described in Chapter 5 do you think would be most helpful? Why?

**3.** What does a cognitive test check?

> **A.** fluid from a person's spinal cord
> **B.** a person's memory and thinking
> **C.** a person's pupils and eye movements

**4.** What happens to a patient with Alzheimer's?

> **A.** Over time, the patient's brain shrinks.
> **B.** Over time, the patient's brain grows.
> **C.** The patient's brain remains exactly the same.

*Answer key on page 32.*

# GLOSSARY

**alertness**
How clear a person's thinking is.

**dementia**
A brain disorder that harms thinking and memory.

**diagnose**
To identify an illness or disease.

**epilepsy**
A brain disorder that causes seizures.

**genetic**
Relating to traits and molecules inherited from parents.

**proteins**
Molecules that are important in telling a living cell what to do.

**radioactive**
Giving off energy that comes from atoms that are breaking apart.

**reflexes**
Actions that happen automatically, without thinking.

**symptoms**
Signs of an illness or disease.

**tumor**
A growth of abnormal tissue in the body.

# TO LEARN MORE

## BOOKS

MacCarald, Clara. *Life with Epilepsy*. Mankato, MN: The Child's World, 2019.

Schwarz, Venessa Bellido. *Medical Technology Inspired by Nature*. Lake Elmo, MN: Focus Readers, 2019.

Silverman, Buffy. *Cutting-Edge Brain Science*. Minneapolis: Lerner Publications, 2020.

## NOTE TO EDUCATORS

Visit **www.focusreaders.com** to find lesson plans, activities, links, and other resources related to this title.

# INDEX

**Answer Key: 1.** Answers will vary; **2.** Answers will vary; **3.** B; **4.** A